TRANCES OF THE BLAST

Mary Ruefle

TRANCES

OF THE

BLAST

Wave Books

Seattle & New York

PUBLISHED BY WAVE BOOKS

WWW.WAVEPOETRY.COM

COPYRIGHT © 2013 BY MARY RUEFLE

WAVE BOOKS TITLES ARE DISTRIBUTED TO THE TRADE BY
CONSORTIUM BOOK SALES AND DISTRIBUTION
PHONE: 800-283-3572 / SAN 631-760X

LIBRARY OF CONGRESS CATALOGING-IN-PUBLICATION DATA
RUEFLE, MARY, 1952–
[POEMS.]
TRANCES OF THE BLAST / MARY RUEFLE. — FIRST EDITION.
P. CM.
ISBN 978-1-933517-73-5 (HARDCOVER: ALK. PAPER)
I. TITLE.
PS3568.U36T73 2013
811'.54—DC23
2012044382

DESIGNED AND COMPOSED BY QUEMADURA
PRINTED IN THE UNITED STATES OF AMERICA

9 8 7 6 5 4 3 2

WAVE BOOKS 038

SAGA

[1]

METAPHYSICAL BLIGHT

[3]

SPIKENARD

[4]

THE ESTATE OF SINGLE BLESSEDNESS

[6]

ARE WE ALONE? IS IT SAFE TO SPEAK?

[7]

LE LIVRE DE MA VIE

[8]

EN ROUTE

[9]

PROVENANCE

[11]

MÜLLER AND ME

[13]

MIDDLE SCHOOL

[15]

FIREWORKS

[16]

COLLEGE

[18]

MIMOSA

[20]

GREETINGS MY DEAR GHOST

[22]

THE DAY

[23]

NEW MORNING

[24]

RECEIVING NEWS OF THE DEVASTATION OF MY MIND

[25]

DONKEY ON

[27]

MIDSUMMER AT JEFFERSON SLOUGH

[29]

JAROSLAV

[30]

GOODNIGHT IRENE

[32]

NITE NITE

[34]

MARCO POLO

[35]

LITTLE ETERNITIES

[36]

FAVORITE SONG

[37]

THE AFTERNOON ACCORDING TO SAINT MATTHEW

[38]

ON VELVET TURF

[39]

PARIS BY MOONLIGHT

[40]

ALBERT FINNEY AGON

[41]

ARGOT

[42]

HELIUM

[43]

APOLOGIA

[45]

HOLD THAT THOUGHT

[46]

ARS POETICA

[49]

SPIDER

[51]

A CUSTOM OF MOURNING

[52]

ABDICATION

[53]

A PENNY FOR YOUR THOUGHTS

[54]

ONE WORLD AT A TIME

[55]

ERIC WITH THE LIGHT BROWN HAIR

[57]

HAPPY

[60]

JUMPING AHEAD

[62]

WOMEN IN LABOR

[64]

SHALIMAR

[66]

TOMORROW WILL BE BEAUTIFUL

[68]

THE BUNNY GIVES US A LESSON IN ETERNITY

[69]

OPEN LETTER TO MY ANCESTORS

[70]

SAWDUST

[72]

BROKEN SPOKE

[73]

FALL LEAF STUDIES

[74]

PLATONIC

[75]

WOODTANGLE

[76]

TRANCES OF THE BLAST

[78]

WHITE BUTTONS

[79]

FASTER LOVE IS ALL THERE IS

[83]

THE SEAFOOD FANCIERS

[85]

CALM, HOW DAREST THOU WAIT

[86]

THE ART OF HAPPINESS

[87]

FOR CARLOS

[88]

LITERAL

[89]

PIPKINS OF THE MIMULUS

[91]

UP ABOVE

[93]

PERIDOT

[94]

NARROW ROAD TO THE NORTH

[95]

WINGS OF LOVE

[97]

DOLOROUS INTERLUDE

[99]

RUMORS OF EARTH

[100]

WHAT WENT YE OUT INTO MAY TO SEE?

[101]

BLOODROOT

[103]

Q & A

[104]

SUDDEN ADDITIONAL ENERGY

[105]

POEM WRITTEN BEFORE I WAS BORN

[107]

ELEGY FOR A GAME

[108]

WITH LOVE & DISREGARD

[109]

PICKING UP PINECONES

[110]

ACKNOWLEDGMENTS

[113]

FOR CHARLIE WRIGHT

GO, AND TAKE THE LITTLE BOOK WHICH IS OPEN
IN THE HAND. TAKE IT, AND EAT IT UP; AND IT
SHALL BE IN THY MOUTH SWEET AS HONEY,
BUT IT SHALL MAKE THY BELLY BITTER.

REVELATION X

TRANCES OF THE BLAST

SAGA

Everything that ever happened to me
is just hanging—crushed
and sparkling—in the air,
waiting to happen to you.
Everything that ever happened to me
happened to somebody else first.
I would give you an example
but they are all invisible.
Or off gallivanting around the globe.
Not here when I need them
now that I need them
if I ever did which I doubt.
Being particular has its problems.
In particular there is a rift through everything.
There is a rift running the length of Iceland
and so a rift runs through every family
and between families a feud.
It's called a saga. Rifts and sagas
fill the air, and beautiful old women
sing of them, so the air is filled with
music and the smell of berries and apples
and shouting when a gun goes off
and crying in closed rooms.
Faces, who needs them?

Eating the blood of oranges
I in my alcove could use one.
Abbas and ammas!
come out of your huts, travel
halfway around the world,
inspect my secret bank account of joy!
My face is a jar of honey
you can look through,
you can see everything
is muted, so terribly muted,
who could ever speak of it,
sealed and held up for all?

METAPHYSICAL BLIGHT

I think it was Saturday my mother was
pregnant with me she could not find
a place to eat the restaurants were crowded
it was the Saturday before Christmas
so she bought a meatpie some fries
a carton of milk from a kiosk
and I became a person.
What if all the cows ate all the grass
and there were no grass?
What if the women were ground
to a Turkish grind for some worthy cause
and there were no women? Without grass
and without women, what could be made?
What could be added to the world?
And the many cows munching in it,
the sound of their manifold munching,
would be as pervasive as a stream
in the not-too-distant.
A world of worried babies without grass,
without women, what would that mean?
You can guess the rest of the story,
how this dear foolish little bit of
Christmas shopping made me lonely,
so lonely even the carton of milk
failed to cause my cracked heart
to sprout a little wheat.

SPIKENARD

Sentence, you always
spoiled my evening.
This is the journal
of my journal.
I used to sniff dill
when things went poorly,
then something snapped inside me.
I plunged my hand in—
after watercress, I guess.
A stream in the middle of me
is not a hospital,
but it takes care of things:
some are dammed,
some let go.
But only after all.
After I had my crying,
I had to indent again.
The scent of spikenard
is nice. It smells of
weird responsibility.
It makes me roll
my stockings down.
I wash my feet with it.

Like pale writing
they lie there on the floor.
I spend more time with my journal
than I spend with myself.
The end.

THE ESTATE OF SINGLE BLESSEDNESS

In this room
we looked naked.
Without a theory,
three eggs in a bowl.
Little by little
we gave up the hope
of ever being understood.
We gave off a big glow.
Outside the window
long-tailed pheasants
swept the forlorn lawns.
Little by little
the house painted by dusk
had its shadow removed.
Monks shot the white hares
at dawn, some of them
ran away and never.
Some of the monks too.

ARE WE ALONE?

IS IT SAFE TO SPEAK?

Dear Unknown Friend,
I know I am real to you,
and though you aren't that real to me
without you I would not exist.
Certainly I would never have stepped
into this nutmeg grater
and become a pile of fine woodsy particles.
It occurs to me we are walking
piles of dust, you and I,
and still it smells as sweet
as summer winds off the coast of Zanzibar
and the sails are up and off we dash
into the brine of our contentment.
I'm glad you know me well.
When I fall asleep, curling up
in a little ball, will you take me home
and hold me in the palm of your hand,
posthumously, anonymously,
and when the time is right
blow me away?

LE LIVRE DE MA VIE

I love you.
But who is the I
and who is the you?

Mr. Potato Head
Mr. Potato Head

Please accept the pressing in
of your eyes.

Here are your glasses.
A book for the evening.

In the book a person
is smiling at you.

Smiling and smiling
like a mother over a baby.

Remove the pipe from your mouth
and smile.

Help me behave,
weeping in the dark earth.

EN ROUTE

On the train with my mother
as soon as it got dark
she turned the light on and
I could see myself perfectly
in the dark glass and I was
startled as I had not much
experience in looking
I noticed my mother barely
glanced at herself and I got
the feeling down pat people
didn't have to look or
maybe they didn't want to
The lady in front of us
had a fur over her shoulder
a little fox with a head
and a tail and two glass beads
embedded where its eyes
would have been
It seemed to comfort her
I thought it was her pet
as I was my mother's
Then the glass eyes of
the animal—fashionable pelt
of the day—met mine and I heard

us—speaking—when my mother
reached up and turned off the light
and I saw the dark hills
and the bare trees and the
tiny innumerable lights
of tiny innumerable towns
while eating a sandwich
without a single scrap
of damp lettuce at the bottom
which had it been there
I would have offered to the fox
or thrown out the window

PROVENANCE

In the fifth grade
I made a horse of papier-mâché
and painted it white
and named it Aurora

We were all going to the hospital
each one with his little animal
to give to the girl who was
lying on her deathbed there
whose name I can't recall

A classmate with freckles perhaps
or such small feet her footsteps
never mattered much

I did not want to give her anything
It seemed unfair she got to ride Aurora
whom I made with my own two hands
and took aside at birth and said *Go*
while I had to walk
perhaps for a very long time

I thought perhaps the animals
would all come back

together and on one day
but they never did

And so I have had to deal with wild
intractable people all my days
and have been led astray in a world
of shattered moonlight and beasts and trees
where no one ever even curtsies anymore
or has an understudy

So I have gone up to the little room
in my face, I am making something
out of a jar of freckles
and a jar of glue

I hated childhood
I hate adulthood
And I love being alive

MÜLLER AND ME

WILHELM MÜLLER, 1794–1827

I am an ordinary fauna, one
who can't remember if a *fife*
is a *rifle* or a *flute*.
After all, there's *strife*
and *fight* in it,
but on the other hand
it's a short sweet word
that rhymes with *life*.
The way the cemetery looks made of books
and the library is a graveyard.
When love frees itself from pain
the angels cut off their wings
and throw them down to earth
(throw in your scarf
to cover my eyes
so your shadow won't wake me).
I'd like to teach
a young starling to speak,
but clearly and distinctly
so his words wouldn't be
like human ones.
I really believed my pain
was not that small,

but how heavy is my happiness

that no sound on earth

can encompass it?

I'm on a fifer's ride

My steed is black and steady

I say goodnight to everyone

To everyone goodmorn

MIDDLE SCHOOL

I went to Cesare Pavese Middle School.
The gymnasium was a chapel dedicated to loneliness
and no one played games.
There was a stained-glass window over the principal's desk
and innumerable birds flew against it,
reciting Shelley with all their might,
but it was bulletproof, and besides,
our leaders were never immortal.
The classrooms were modeled after motel rooms,
replete with stains, and in remedial cases
saucers of milk on the floor for innumerable cats,
or kittens, depending on the time of year.
In them we were expected to examine ourselves and pass.
The principal himself once jumped off the roof
at noon, to show us school spirit.
Our mascot was Twist-Tie Man.
Our team the Bitter Herbs.
Our club the Reconsiderers.
It was an honor to have gone,
though a tad strict in retrospect.
You have probably heard that we all became janitors,
sitting in basements next to boilers
reading cheap paperback books of Italian poetry,
and never sweep a thing.
Yet the world runs fine.

FIREWORKS

The world was designed and built
to overwhelm and astonish.
Which makes it hard to like.
Like, an American is someone
who thinks Jan Vermeer is from Vermont,
and a woman. I am a woman from Vermont.
Little less surprising than the copiousness
of transpiration, which is so inconsequential
I cannot live without it. Later I will look
for a nail paring on the floor,
as if a maid were coming tomorrow
(one always has to pick up first).
Right now I am writing
on the back of a bank statement.
My happiness is marred only
by my failure to attain it.
Otherwise it would astonish and overwhelm.
Quick, children, put on your robes,
we must all go downstairs to see something.
On this same night was Balthazar
murdered by his servants:
what the Russian soldier, quoting
Heine, scratched on the wall in the room
where the whole royal family was shot,

shot to fleshy pieces with many aims,
at least twenty of which left
explosive stars in the wallpaper.
Their greed and power astonished all.
Their death overwhelms us.

COLLEGE

Tom opened three packets of white sugar
and with the confidence of a conductor
dumped them on his cake.
Phoebe wrapped a towel around her head
and began singing Faulkner.
We didn't know Joel mowed lawns for a living
so we guessed his paintings were mountains
not gigantic blades of grass.
Eugenia told again the story of being born Eugenia.
Clearly I was in the wrong place,
clearly I did not belong there,
my only complaint being my go was completely gone
plus a condition of the eye in which
water accumulates and tends to run over the margin.
True, I'd tried living among mosses
and their kin, liverwort and earthworms,
but in general I knew how to rotisserate chickens
and purse my thoughts.
I didn't believe bridges could repair themselves,
I wasn't born Jack Benny. Poor Eugenia!
There I was, a tiki in the place where products go
to become 75 percent more minty.
For it is lonely to walk through beauty
when you are young, and an earthly failure,

and the imperial sunshine has not yet crowned.

The night before graduation our party

took a short stroll in the moonlight

when Joel began to cry. The grass,

he said, it's made of *catgut*.

Tom gave him a packet of sugar.

Phoebe remarked his tears looked like skiers

streaking down the mountainside.

Eugenia told the story of being born Eugenia.

And I, I would not go near the sea for nearly thirty years,

I would not drink tea for another twenty,

I would not undress, use pockets, read Walter Benjamin

or listen to a bumblebee even if he bent

the right wing of my scarlet runner,

modeling myself after a woman

who could only say one thing at a time,

and found herself one day in hell,

where she went casually and without

purpose, having read every poem

ever written, and finding not a single one

even remotely sad enough.

MIMOSA

FOR JAMES SCHUYLER

Pink dandruff of some tree
afloat on the swimming pool.
What's that bird?
I'm not from around here.
My mail will probably be forwarded
as quietly as this pink fluff
or a question or morphine
or impatience or a mistake
or the infinite method
established by experience
but never in this world.
I've always wanted to use
malarkey and *henna* in a poem
and now I have.
Oh Jimmy, all you ever wanted
was to see the new century
but no such luck.
You never saw a century plant
either, or you would have
taken another drink.
They grow for one hundred years,
bloom in their centenary spring
then die forevermore.

The stalk is ten feet tall
(you'd be jealous) rising
out of a clump of cactus leaves
(think yucca) then busting into
creamy ovoids flaming
on the candelabrum.
I was in an air-conditioned car
when I saw it but still felt
the heat of its beauty,
I wanted to stop and talk to it
but we sped on, so tonight
I'll xanax myself to sleep
with the sweet thought that
today and every day is a
century plant of its own
seeded awful long beginning
blooming in drive-by yelps
of love and helplessness
and you saw plenty of them,
spectacular and sad as
a head of hennaed hair,
a lot of malarkey
if you ask anybody
other than us.

GREETINGS MY DEAR GHOST

One thing life has taught me
is that even dolls have bad days,
days when the wind presents its challenges,
you open your mouth, it gets full of grit,
cars are mangled, people are injured,
the Four Noble Truths sealed in a capsule
and sent into space, snowballs
hurled over a few daffodils startle
the piano keys out of their sleep.
Morning, I have just come from there,
they throw big pieces of it down with a smash.
When my doll refuses to speak I say Go, go
where the high, blinding, stately magnificence
of reality is being taught, but not even
a wandering little drift of unidentified sound
comes from her mouth, her face is haunted
in a bloodcurdling way, but that is her way,
her way of saying
How sweetly human, the April air.

THE DAY

Describe the day when you first knew
that you were Real.
Okay, then describe the day
when you first had the sensation
life was but a Dream.
Well then, the day little Donald
took your jar of buttons
and you wept under the aspens
who did not seem to care one way or another
which made you madder than a hornet
and when Mrs. Felton saw you
stinging yourself, she invited you in
and gave you a glass of milk
and a piece of pie. What Kindness.
What kind of pie?
Did its purple eyes tell you then
what you know now?

NEW MORNING

I smell the cream
before I put it in my coffee
because I never want to suffer
like that again as long as I live,
it was unbearable, no one should
have to suffer like that, not the
littlest animal, ever, I can recall
my mouth so contorted with pain
I was down on the floor
if there had been someplace lower
I would have gone there
it was unspeakable the way
I was an animal then
though I had always been one
it was a declension of that
and in some place no bigger than
the plastic thimble the cream comes in
when they give it to you in public,
a place so deep inside me it could be
its own organ if they could find it,
I felt this suffering to be an act—
never unreal, not that—
but performed by another
while I watched, helpless and shocked,
unable to stop what was happening.

RECEIVING NEWS OF THE
DEVASTATION OF MY MIND

A baby swan brought the news,
dragging his brown feathers
over the cobblestones.
Because I naturally stoop
none of my attendants
thought to water me.
Later that evening, after
the revelry, in which the swan
was rewarded richly (and later
placed in an orphanage for
the kind) a few bold souls
stayed on and helped me
finish the initial "Z"
in the embroidered manuscript
my bedspread had become.
Tucked between its covers
I lay for forty days, naked
and alone, composing a deposition
of my sole remaining memory,
the baby swan as he waddled forward,
shedding down.
From this position I will never move.
When I open my mouth

a bubble floats out,
and I am in it, and all of my
lifelong friends, the stars,
the wandering stars, who follow
the migration of birds, and who
follow the news, the migration
of news, until they cannot remember
the half of it.

DONKEY ON

When I am alone I make a sound
the lord does not understand.
Then he makes the sound of a helicopter receding.
Then my sound goes after his sound.

My sound sounds like an ordinary bowl of oatmeal
that can sometimes be almost liquid
and sometimes effect a crust.

His sound is small and bitter,
capable of great strength
and universal flowering,
as if the world will never stop expanding
once helicopters are gone.

Of course, I can only make one sound a year
so sometimes it sounds like
Please guess what I want to tell you

And he says
Without a mother it would be good to know English?

And I press this question into a photograph album
without a comma,

which is severely inadequate to the task of
reconstructing a life.

So I say
Perhaps I am too handmade?

And he says
It is spring, I am the peppermint king!

And then he does something generous:
he drops me a private year
wrapped in plastic,
tied up with string.

The only question is how to spend it,
so I carry it on my back
like a mule bringing ice cream
to the sun.

MIDSUMMER AT JEFFERSON SLOUGH

A few stumbles, then, as far as paths go, ok.
Noon has broken,
morning has been.
Terrible mounds of spirals
are upon us.
So-and-so has said it better—
there's not much left for us to twirl.
The terrible moment of truth comes next.
Take my hand.
I shall show you where I live.
All the summers of my life
have been lived here,
in the darkened halls
of Natural History.
This is my diorama.
Here is my heron. He is waiting for fish.
They will never come.
Here are the real grasses lying still,
drifting in front of a painted sky.
It is as close to July
as I will ever come.
Perhaps I am of the earth denied.
What a drag. Oh well,
I have enough ideas.
Do you? Do you?

JAROSLAV

I, I mean you, I mean the shadow
of your shadow—
it's been a long time since I
said the word *buttercup*.
If you are trying to sleep
may the sheep fall down
all around you
till you stand like a pillar
in the billowing mist
of their woolly backs.
Pillar, I wonder how you will see this year.
Will you speak quietly to no one
at a great distance? Will you be
surpassed by the sound of wind and rain?
There is something about pillars
that leads me to believe they are
real people, with hair, having
conversations. Even in ruins,
at intervals, like telephone poles.
I don't know if we are ever really
finally torn from the spot,
but I remain on this earth
to grow at your feet, Jaroslav.
To be your buttercup,

I remain.
Oh what a lonely head
would say such a thing
and then repeat it,
indefinitely.

GOODNIGHT IRENE

I think the tree is very much turned on
I can feel its sticky sap rising in my eyes
Its sticky sap is in my eyes
I do not think the tree wishes it were dead
I think the baby is very much turned on
Look baby a birdie in the tree
Say bye-bye birdie now go out and get a job
My job is writing poems and reading them to a cloud
I think the clouds are very much turned on
Apparently birds are very much turned on
when they fly through the clouds
and come out shedding water from their wings
Even when the earth was flat it was very much turned on
I do not think the earth wishes it were dead
I do not think the baby wishes it were dead either
I think god was very much turned on
when he set up his easel and began painting the ether
Anyone who looks can see the pinks and blues are turned on
I think Leadbelly was very much turned on
I think Irene was very much turned on
When they looked at the painting
they wanted to leave the party together
Is that a cloud?
I think questions are very much turned on

That is why they go serpentine at the end

I do not think the questions wish they were dead

I think the idea of a centillion is very much turned on

But there are darkables in a centillion questions

As when a dead face asks for a kiss

Oh Oh the glorified chloroform of the air

And the trees and the little nest at the top of the leaves

I think the idea of leaving is pretty much turned on

Why do *you* wish you were dead?

NITE NITE

None of the dolls could sleep.
The braided rug dreamt of being
a traveling companion.
The snow stopped, briefly,
on its way past the window.
The mother and father did not
touch each other, but each felt
they could hear laughter coming
from China, and the child felt
knocked by the earth,
and though she was blind
and would always be blind,
one day she would tap blindly
with her white-tipped stick,
wearing orange high heels.

MARCO POLO

a faint memory
when quite young
believed it made
all the difference

a faint memory
old, wrapped in a shawl
bewildered and half-asleep
sat near the bed
but did not speak

what difference
could it make now?

a faint memory
finally dozed
and dreamt
of playing with kids
half its age

none of them had ever seen before
a pile of bobby pins on the side of the pool

LITTLE ETERNITIES

When are we happiest? he asked her.
Not one of them could get the seats
to go back, not one of them really knew
what was in the glove box, though
everything there was theirs.

When they got to where they were going,
a park, a gray squirrel came jumping along.
Childhood! It was in one of the houses nearby.
Money! Every day it seemed to loose itself
from its lurking-place and drift away.

So he smelled the underside
of his own arm. And the squirrel
paused, one of those little eternities
never mentioned again.

FAVORITE SONG

My life.
Is a passing September
no one will recall.
She crooned.
The riparian leads to the littoral.
Like a horse ridden to death.
I saw my life in knickerbockers.
I saw the inside of its locker.
It hung a mirror there.
I saw it shaving its face.
I saw its face in a lather.
Like a horse ridden to death.
Heaven provided us with tears.
We rub them around. We share them.
We think they are tadpoles.
We think they will grow up
into beautiful singing things.
But they won't.
I saw the earth was one of the great
unsuccessful poems.

THE AFTERNOON ACCORDING

TO SAINT MATTHEW

There's the black truck
with orange flames
on its hood. There's the girl
in the pink pajamas. There's her sister
in a bumblebee suit.
They are playing with dirt.
When they find bugs
they scream
but no one hears them.
Their minds are growing though.
In the late afternoon light
they scoop the dirt into tin cans
so they can bury it
in the backyard.
I think we have a case
of two women grinding at the mill—
one will be taken and one
will be left,
but it's way too early
to tell.

ON VELVET TURF

I dash outdoors so I will know
a little more about the day—
I stride forth filled with the whiff.
What's to know is always a little to the left,
deep in the vine-covered hole of a hedgehog down
by the mossy stump. If something is impaled down there
I want to know. I don't mind throwing myself
into the cistern of the Middle Ages.
Who knows, here once the embattled farmers stood,
their gallant foreheads broadly glistening.
I've read whole books standing up naked.
I've bragged all my life of the glories
I had in common with the rest of the world,
glories that fled through the windfields
and raked rivers, through the sere leaves
of the trees—
now that the broken gravy boat will sail no more
and the electric fence electrify no one,
now that the crepitating rain has come
and the winter lilt departed, it is time
to come out of my hole—
though the stars take me back
more than I am willing to admit.

PARIS BY MOONLIGHT

Oh my god, it's Paris by moonlight
Even the trees are drunk and walking
A single pink slipper floats down the Seine
What kind of trees are those?
Those are trees in Paris by moonlight
What size is that slipper?
It is the exact size of the sole
We ate in the little restaurant an hour ago
Under the trees in Paris by moonlight
There is no end to our painlessness
The trees will never find it
The slipper never reach it
Morning after morning the smell of coffee
Makes them nauseous
While we go on painlessly in Paris
Barefoot and swaggering
Our aluminum heads in the moon glow so
We are like an advertisement
For those who will come after us
Anyone can see without French
They should just stay in bed

ALBERT FINNEY AGON

There he is, twenty-two years old,
he's knocked up some girl
and they are going to the abortionist.
He's so handsome we could wash his feet.
When he shoots that old lady
in the ass with his slingshot
then runs down the alley
we are waiting with our bucket.

Half a century later,
a truly dented face.
Looking down it,
we wonder if he's inside.
It's a serious thing, muttering.
He drags on his fag
then throws it in the street.
He turns the collar of his raincoat up.
It isn't even raining.
It's nowadays. Nowadays
he dies at the end of every film.

ARGOT

The moon passes her twentieth night.
Month after month, she dies so young.
What are the trout thinking?
At dawn on the thirteenth
I am lost in the great expanse
of tiny thoughts.
When I say trout I mean you.

HELIUM

You are helium. You make everything rise.
You are so precious the gods quarrel over you.
They invented time for you. When you didn't
like it, they broke the hands from the clock
so you could write. They invented Esperanto
for you, but you didn't like that either
so went out and wept bitterly, for which they
turned your tears into Sprite, because men
and women are easily bored by the passage of time
and the facts of life and need a fountain.
A large part of your problem is death,
which is lifeless and unhelpful. Night returns
to stay another night. Even the unconscious
mollusks are conscious of that. And the drama
of bloodroot—teeny flowers falling apart,
gigantic leaf growing all summer—gods everywhere
with different ideas. They invented color
for you, which split into colors, all of which
ended up in little numbers dispersed throughout
what is now called the living room. And still
you are in shambles, and lie down and levitate
for the happy futile future. O Sheer One,
they made you in different combinations
in different directions so you could retell

the diaspora of exasperation. They gave you
a dibble. They made you wrists. They made you
the germ of an idea, one would think it would
be greatly in the idea's way—
yet the heart hanging in the pear tree
is finally cut down. You did everything
with your own two hands.

APOLOGIA

I used to love to kneel down and pray for the bud
but now that the chestnuts are empty
I have not combed my hair in years.
The days of my nights are gone
and my only friends
are the moon and rabbits.
You never heard me speak.
I never talked.
I might have been a great question.
Instead, I have been the secret weather,
the servant who refused to wash,
the one who ate an orange
then sat in the corner
sewing the skins back together.
Call me unkempt. A pip
in a rotten pomegranate.
A pip in a world of pips.
There is no need to get excited.
If you saw my face in a bowl
you would not wake it anytime soon.
Remember me, your servant,
who was not yet used to being alive,
and was always surprised
by the dear, stupid days
wearing stripes
and bearing the faces of those she loved.

HOLD THAT THOUGHT

I sit sometimes in the dark,
and for that you will think
I am selfish, I live in the dark
and I work in the dark, I eat in
the dark, I am writing this without
light, but one thing I will not do
is love you in the dark. To all ye
who sleep, it is raining in the alley,
I hear the laughter turn into an
argument, the world is saturated
and full of misty tricks, I am
perhaps myself a misty trick
of the dark and for that you
will think I am no one, you can
dream of the potato blight if you want,
the night is dark and the knife
is dark, and Walt Whitman loves me,
Walt walks down to the sea and my
Edwardian earrings are of no help
to him now, he goes in, toothless,
hairless, and without rings our
feelings will never be identified,
he expectorates into the sea

and his spit gives off a faint blue
light like that of the moon, everything
he does he does in order to see,
he likes looking at the world, why not,
born into a body like that, a body
that is lonely and scared and probably
angry, but it is his body and he loves it
to the extent of the Mongol Empire,
just as I love yours, hold that thought
I have finally spoken—
I love you more than George Sand loved
Alfred de Musset, I love you more than
George Sand loved Pietro Pagello, I
love you more than George Sand loved
Frédéric Chopin, it makes the brain
swell, it is dark in there, the cells
die by the hundreds, they die by the
thousands, it could be Abe Lincoln's
war, every creature crawling all over
the planet has one, yours can walk down
to the sea, yours can go in, have you
ever thought about standing naked in
the rain like Walt did, it is dark
but not too late, it is raining in
the alley, Bob Dylan isn't a big talker

but he looked at everything real close
for an hour, your own mother has a
picture of you in her wallet,
even if you are asleep I bet
you're not dreaming of that.

ARS POETICA

You go through the past
and there is a wall, and some steps
down; you come into a lane and go
until there is no more lane, but only
a path, and then you come to a field
that must have been a garden once
with a house or something.

It was only an old place
where nobody lived.
I said whose was it,
but he didn't know,
and I said why didn't somebody
live there, but he didn't know that
either, he said it was art.

He said I am tired
of pointing out to the dandelions
how beautiful this world is—

so our hair walked around the garden
and saw things growing
and was confused and sobbed.

It was only an old place where nobody lived.
Some butterflies flitting around—
memories with nothing to do.
We thought we might carry one back.

Look, he said, nothing remains of anybody,
everything is aimless here.
We wanted to follow a flying squirrel
to the home of time, but everything
exploded into fuzz.

We knew whose it was.

SPIDER

The spider can barely walk, his legs are so scared—
he's got to get from the bar of soap to the uppermost
showerstall tile that is his home, and he has suffered
a betrayal so great he's lost in his own neighborhood,
crawling on his hands and knees, so to speak, in and out
of the shadows of other tiles he's passed before but
barely recognizes, given his state of shock and disbelief.
Spiders don't hear very well—he can't hear the rain
as it falls and cools his flaming legs, the distant screams
of another's crisis mean nothing to him, he can't hear
his own heartbeat, an alarm casting his skeleton straight
into hell, his blood ignited by the bellows of loss.
If the gods implore him to hold his saliva, he doesn't
hear them, he goes on crawling toward the one safe spot,
which has become, in his mind, the destination of his life
and this night rolled into one, a wet bag at the bottom
of which, were it to fall, would lie his demise—
too awful to discuss.

A CUSTOM OF MOURNING

I wore blood on my clothes for three days.
I used my initials, never my name.
I would not cut the grass
nor make repairs
no matter an outbuilding
or mechanical failure.
I did not eat eggs
as they are a sign of life
yet grew the border on my stationery
to three inches wide,
vastly restricting the space to write in.
I read not the news
nor old books
nor the backs of cans.
Everything was heated haphazardly.
As I had vowed,
the mirrors were covered with beautiful cloth.
My hair grew to fathoms
and the soles of my shoes
were made of leaves.
And when at last the thirty years did pass,
I too hated the end of summer,
and bitterly.

ABDICATION

With all its little blobs,
Napoleon's signature
looks like it rained all year (it did).
On the island of solitaire
there is a game:
you place your hand on your chest
and speak.
You can feel the poetry rotting
in your stomach.
You know with absolute certainty
reality is the thing turned toward you.
Day after day
you know what's for lunch:
another lamb.
A stinky red wet affair
born in the blood that falls from the skies.
But how surprised you are
when a book arrives,
or a new pair of gloves,
and I suppose, being forced to admit it,
there is a scrap of delight
when the page comes bearing a pillow.
Here, on the pillow, are the dead bees—
two lions who fooled around in spring.

A PENNY FOR YOUR THOUGHTS

How are we to find eight short English words
that actually stand for autumn?
One peculiar way to die of loneliness
is to try. Pretend November has
a sliver of ice in her throat.
Pretend it is nice, pretend the sliver
of ice is nice, and beckons you.
Talk for half an hour about the little churchyard
full of the graves of people who have died
eating nachos. Go on until you can go no further brown.
Let the river flow. It is written in stone.
Let the sparrows take your only coin
and fly with it, twittering over some main event.
What color ribbon will you wear in your hair?
Now the clouds look burnt. But first they burned.
To you I must tell all or lie.

ONE WORLD AT A TIME

I wanted to starch my own headdress.
I wanted my fingers to smell always of laundry.

I wanted the sounds of my shoes
to echo down the long corridors.

I wanted to approach the dying soldier,
freshly bandaged in his iron bed,
and lay my hands on his head.

Somewhere unseen a musician practicing
for the evening's recital.

Those sounds filling in for words,
filling up our unspoken love.

But in the end I didn't care who died.
I wasn't even willing to mop up the blood.

I put his soup bowl to my lips.
Who put my thoughts in alphabetical order?

They were forced to circle at night,
just to make ends meet.

And my pith helmet filled with sand—
the encryptions crested and slumped,
always advancing.

In the endless desert of eyes
even the stars were a mirage.

I loved my camel though,
and leaning forward
hugged him on.

ERIC WITH THE LIGHT BROWN HAIR

I have no horse! I have no horse!

cries Eric sitting on the porch
of the Twin Maples Retirement Home

and it's a fine spring day,
I am walking to the playground
when I stop to hear this,
the most profound moment our town
has seen since the ice-cream truck
adopted a rendition of Stephen Foster's
Oh! Susanna

the profundity of which should be apparent
to all those who linger in blissful repose
over the sad lives of great and forgotten men

I have no horse! I have no horse!

Eric behaves as one does
after a beheadment

and I love the ology of it
and the ism of his cry

I love the ology of clouds

and the ism of rain too

but not as specifically as
I love Eric, who seeks his red rose
in the fume of the moment,
his mouth oily and explosive,
wide open, waiting for someone
to throw a few peanuts in

God has made some pretty weird comments
in his time, about the nature of human
life and all of that, naturally
they are profound

but somehow they seem like a morbid imitation
compared to Eric's

and even if he goes back centuries
every time he gets stewed

like the wildflowers who wither on the shore
far from our native glen

I sigh for Eric, who I unanswered,
I sigh for Eric who once had light brown hair

as I swing
floating like a vapor
on the soft-spoken air

HAPPY

After my mother died
I could hear her in the attic
playing with dolls.
I could see through things, like air
and scum.
It was wonderful—
I got to clean the earth
on my hands and knees, I got to wax it!
When it was shiny I went ice-skating
in the middle of the night.
I was happy out there
skating under the moon
with no one else around.
I felt so happy I started sewing
clothes for the moon.
Tiny things at first,
like christening gowns for caterpillars.
And my mother bought them!
She was so happy to see me so happy
it hardly mattered we had never
spoken much on Earth.
I'd always been one of those morose, silent
types, who couldn't conceive of getting ahead.
And now I'm happy. I'm so happy

that the next time I see my dad
in a black cape up in a tree
throwing messages down,
I'm going to fly a kite
with his face on it.

JUMPING AHEAD

I ought to have been an otter, that's obvious.
I ought to have been a dress
passed down through three generations
then ripped in strips and used to oil the harpsichord
and then the hinges of the medicine cabinet
before being tossed on a fire
where six kids on their knees
are roasting marshmallows.
I wish I were a graham cracker.
Whether I exist or not—I wish
I knew that. Oh tremendous mystery
of what I'm doing for dinner tonight.
If I had had two glass eyes
could the ocean have seen
I was his distant cousin?
I wish I'd said god instead of ocean
but then I'd be ashamed of my thoughts.
I ought not to have named each one Mimi.
If only I'd understood that loneliness
was just loneliness, only loneliness
and nothing more.
But I was blind.
Little did I know.
If only I'd invented salt.

I might have died happy.
I wish I loved you,
but you can't have everything.
I ought to have had bizarre erroneous beliefs.
If only I'd had gigantic forelegs attached to my legs
I'd have leapt off the edge
every time I came to the edge of you.

WOMEN IN LABOR

Women who lie alone at midnight
because there is no one else to lie to

Women who lie alone at midnight
at noon in the laundromat
destroying their own socks

Women who lie alone at midnight:
Hans Brinker, or The Silver Skates

Women who lie alone at midnight
as the first furl of starlight
purls the moon with nacre

Women who lie alone at midnight
sending a postcard bearing
the face of a bawling infant
who cries *I am for the new!*

Women who lie alone at midnight
reciting the names of shoes

Women who lie alone at midnight
spurting unjustified tears,

the kind that run sideways
never reaching the mouth,
the kind you cannot swallow

Women who lie alone at midnight
singing *breast away the burden of my tender*
and afterwards burp

Women who lie alone at midnight
obeying the laws of physics
Women who let their dreams curl at the end
Women in a monastery of flamingos

Women who die alone at midnight
contributing to the end, to
lost time, to the rain and flies,
seeing the bird they saw trapped in the airport
surviving by the water fountain

What's more, try it sometime
It works

SHALIMAR

God put his finger on my sacrum
and he lifted me, he set me
in the center of the universe,
the curious desire
of my chronically lonely life.

It was cold and dark and lonely
and I was scared.

There were no accessories.
I burst into tears over nothing.

What would Jimmy Schuyler do?
WWJSD?

And as quietly as the sound of Kleenex
being pulled from a box,
I sneezed.

And morning, that goddess,
as if she were slightly deaf,
barely lifted her head off the horizon
before lying back down.

And a rose opened her portals
and the scent ran up an elephant's trunk,
or tried to.

Such a long way for everything to travel!

From here I look like a front moving in.

An icy purple light
a poet would say belonged to a perfume stopper
belonging to his mother.

When it was her nipple.

You know, neither in the past
or in the future.

TOMORROW WILL BE BEAUTIFUL

Time kissed me goodbye
and moved into a car without wheels
abandoned in a field.
I guess the little things
just ate him.
When autumn came I wondered
if he had a bag of almonds,
left him some shoes by the aspen
but he never took them.
When the blizzard came,
every fifteen minutes
he got out and cleaned
the windshield with his hands,
which gave me hope.
And then he just seemed
to slip away
and then he was just
the shadow of a submarine
moving inside
that hulk of ice.

THE BUNNY GIVES US
A LESSON IN ETERNITY

We are a sad people, without hats.

The history of our nation is tragically benign.

We like to watch the rabbits screwing in the graveyard.

We are fond of the little bunny with the bent ear

who stands alone in the moonlight

reading what little text there is on the graves.

He looks quite desirable like that.

He looks like the center of the universe.

Look how his mouth moves mouthing the words

while the others are busy making more of him.

Soon the more will ask of him to write their love

letters and he will oblige, using the language

of our ancestors, those poor clouds in the ground,

beloved by us who have been standing here for hours,

a proud people after all.

OPEN LETTER TO MY ANCESTORS

Sometimes I walk around the house
wearing a green clay mask
it's supposed to be for my skin
but I don't care about that
I wear it in honor of you
I am so sadly far away from you
I secretly hope someone rings the doorbell
so they cannot recognize me
Surprise! I am seasick
on my long voyage
I've left everything behind
except this valise
which I protect with my body
and God's love because I believe
in the day I will board a bus
with a bag of potatoes in my right hand
worth more than the valise
and everything in it
Thank you for that
These smoked chops are incredible
You have to look at it as one person
with a very long life
it's better that way
blood, tears, violence, hate, ashes, everything

the mad blue terror of dying
of having to learn another language
Perdurabo
it all works out in time
there is no end
I had no kids
there's a niece in Cincinnati
she's marrying a Greek next week
just so you know
I'm going to wash you off now
into the luminous depths
where even a recluse bird must fly

SAWDUST

Long before Mickey Mouse,
long before his Creators
added gloves so his hands
wouldn't terrify us,
long before today's afternoon
when I was trying to take
a nail out of the wall
and it wouldn't stop coming
so I screamed
how much more of you can there be?
Jesus was a kid
playing with a bent nail
in his father's shop
when a small amount of fascinating blood
started coming out of his thumb
so he turned to his dog
a puppy really
and offered the thumb to be licked—
without a word from anyone
just like that
not one adult around
to start screaming—

BROKEN SPOKE

You grow old.
You love everybody.
You forgive everyone.
You think: we are all leaves
dragged along by a wheel.
Then comes a splendid spotted
yellow one—ah, distinction!
And in that moment
you are dragged under.

FALL LEAF STUDIES

I wake up, I count my money,
then I have lunch.
After lunch I go
to the window.
The leaves are no longer green.
When the leaves fall,
at the end of summer,
who knows if there are enough
to cover the ground?
Do they themselves
ever actually really *know?*
They come down slowly
and with many conjectures
after all that yak
and in that bronzed state
they pause.

PLATONIC

Did it mean anything? The stone, the rose,
darkness, wood, wind, flame, the violin.
The practical man, the visible world,
the painted ponies, the sea, the wilderness
of cellophane, my last word, my crumpled message
to my friend? Was I in search of something,
tools maybe, or seeds, for many odd things
are stowed under the overthinking.
Let's begin to talk about things,
and what they should be named,
and whether it will be necessary
to draw any of them.
The sound of the teakettle—
it was the most terrible thing in the world.
Sometimes it was a wolf, and sometimes
a man or a woman, whatever it felt like,
even falling cherry blossoms, and always
it could take you out, and then it did,
leaving the whole room as impressive
as an unexplored cave.

WOODTANGLE

I remember the king passed massive amounts
of inarticulate feeling into law.
I envied all the beautiful things.
Sometimes I called my own name.
I cursed myself why do I have so many
strange questions. I tried to cram myself
with the gentler things so as to release
some suppressed inclination. My name is
Woodtangle. I remember my mother
when she wore yellow was beautiful
like a finch and then she died. I remember
thinking my father was mean but knowing he
was kind. I remember thinking my father was
kind but knowing he was mean. I remember thinking
all things made of themselves examples of the
same thing. And Everyman the next day would follow.
I remember thinking the world ended a long time ago
but no one noticed. I remember every dinner
at Vespaio with Tomaz and the Saturday night
the antique cars paraded by for an hour
and I couldn't breathe for the fumes and I was happy.
I remember thinking the sexual significance of
everything seemed absurd because we are made of

time and air (who cares) and then I remembered
the day the king passed massive amounts of inarticulate
feeling into law he threw a cherry bomb into the crowd
and I thought it was fruit and I ate it.

TRANCES OF THE BLAST

Alarming brightness of yellow speech

Transparency of all hearts

Everyone I know is in a speck of danger

The head is in the blood

What is the code for happiness?

Blackberries forever

At one time

Now it is another time

How near we were to having thoughts

How near we are today

Whole words, ashamed, apart, by themselves, transfigured

And if by chance that makes you happy

Explain yourself or vanish

WHITE BUTTONS

Having been blown away
by a book
I am in the gutter
at the end of the street
in little pieces
like the alphabet
(Mother do not worry
letters are not flesh
though there's meaning in them
but not when they are mean
my letters to you were mean
I found them after you died
and read them and tore them up
and fed them to the wind
thank you for intruding
I love you now leave)
Also at the end of the street
there is a magnolia tree
the white kind
that tatters
after it blooms
so the tree winds up
in the street
Our naked shivering bodies

must be at some distance
missing us come back
come back they cry
come home
put down that book
whenever you read
you drift away on a raft
you like your parrot
more than you like me
and stuff like that
(dear Father
you always were a bore
but I loved you more
than interesting things
and in your honor
I've felt the same about myself
and everyone I've ever met)
I like to read in tree houses
whenever I can which is seldom
and sometimes never
The book that blew me away
held all the problems
of the world
and those of being alive
under my nose
but I felt far away from them

at the same time

reading is like that

(I am sorry I did not

go to your funeral

but like you said

on the phone

an insect cannot crawl

to China)

Here at the end of the street

the insects go on living

under the dome

of the pacific sky

If Mary and Joseph

had walked the sixty miles

to Bethlehem vertically

they would have found

themselves floating

in the outer pitch of space

it would have been cold

no inns

a long night

in the dark endless

and when they began to cry

the whole world would think

something had just been born

I like to read into things

as I am continually borne forward
in time by the winds like the snow
(dear Sister
you were perfect in every way
like a baby
please tell Brother
the only reason
we never spoke
was out of our great love
for each other
which made a big wind
that blew us apart)
I think I am coming back
I feel shoulders
where a parrot could land
though a tree would be
as good a place as any
You cannot teach a tree to talk
Trees can say   it is spring
but not   though bright sunlight
can also be very sad
have you noticed?

FASTER LOVE IS ALL THERE IS

There is nothing faster than more faster love
faster love is all there is
as it is 4:03 and life takes another
amazing and distressful turn
as when a seagull
picks up a French fry
and becomes human

What are we to do at sea
with our logarithms
when faster love is all there is

When April has forty-six days
after which it can't go on
floating on the mattress
so it rises so we can see
the flowers it was once upon
and a few strands of brownish hair

When we tiptoe down the hall for ice
When ice falls out of the shoot and into the bucket
When a cube falls through the grate and is gone

When we huddle in our sea of cars
When we suffer muchly from glare in the face

and keep the eyes alive
with nothing more than an eyedropper

When we never went snorkeling
but nonetheless sensed people
are more capable of floating by
than any other creature

Stop stop pretty water
Raise a cup of kindness to them
As it is there's nothing faster
Faster love, it's all there is

THE SEAFOOD FANCIERS

The boat, the bait,
the frozen fish,
the boat butcher
washing the guts off his face.

The little cyclone of blood
in the drain.

The man in the glittery suit
spraying cologne in his mouth.

The restaurant,
the candlelight,
the air bubbles in the champagne,
the look in her eyes of the sea
and the stars over the sea.

The starfish who have babies
every night, that's why there are
so many of them, wailing overhead,
waiting to be fed.

CALM, HOW DAREST THOU WAIT

Those flowers look so happy together
The tragic in his pink coat
brushing through the gossamer
tries with all his skill
to get his clothes dirty
but really those flowers
look so happy together
They are not questions left howling
because their owner has died
They do not engage a private tutor
who teaches them how to live for a thousand years
then die in their sleep
They are not innumerable birds
lost in the soft dark late September air
They do not distinguish between
the general wreckage and the singular wreckage
They are not faithful scholars of zero
seated in a circle
They are not instructions for the little thread
should the needle appear again
They are not even entwined
They just stand next to each other
in the churchyard silence
and from time to time
help the rain
by listening to it

THE ART OF HAPPINESS

I am too weak to speak,
that is why I am writing this—
will you please bring me some water?
I cannot make the few feet to the sink,
the art of happiness prevents me.
When you bring me the water
make sure it is in a glass.
Water would rather be held by a glass
than be in a stream on its way to the ocean.
That is the art of happiness.
Alas it will one day leave the glass
but water would rather be held by the body
than be in a stream on its way to the ocean.
Alas it will one day leave the body
but not to worry now.
That is the art of happiness.
When water enters us it becomes
delirious, it gets to push things out of its way,
it gets to form an opinion and then express it,
it gets to see what no one else has seen.
As you can see I am dying of happiness.
Please ask the surgeon to come
and remove this day—
I don't want to die of happiness.
What's a glass of water to you?
What's a phone call or two?

FOR CARLOS

Scattered stars,

and the red light of each bell.

If you are in love,

no one can hear you.

If you are squeezing the throat of a rabbit

until it fits in your silver ring,

no one can hear you.

If you are alone with no other company

but that of an old book, if you are telling

the parable of a dozen roses,

the universe shines in splendor

with the silence of fish,

the red glow of the earth below

could be the last chip of nail polish

left on the right hand of your little sister,

whom you kissed, not hearing

the acetone of your own breath.

Everything sells later for nothing.

In the woods, by the mill, without help, of silver.

In the grass, by the pond, without subtitles, the splash.

Dog barking, baby crying, object

falling, boys laughing, woman sobbing.

Burning stars, no one can hear you—

hair is blowing out the car window.

LITERAL

Yesterday as I sat driving past a field
I saw a school of children
with insect nets.
They moved very delicately over the grass
in their hunt for the future.
I think they were modern.
Basically I am killing
myself with cigarettes
because in the fifth grade
the square-dance teacher
made me sit one out.
None of this will help a baby to grow—
but ticks can kill you.
This is the junk of everyday life.
Let us flee from it.
I am old.
The breeze is too strong for me.
It is no longer possible to stand up.
I like to smell stones.
There is a whiff of snow in them.
In snow there is the scent of shadows.
Stones casting shadows on snow—
there are no nerves in that.
Now I am watching my secret thoughts

lest they escape.
Now you are following me, are you not?
Now you are with me.
Let us take off our shoes
and walk in the snow.
It does not happen every day.

PIPKINS OF THE MIMULUS

I am sitting at my desk practicing
the footstepping of a mouse
who departs without having found the pear.
I am unlettyrde with broun hayre
and have sympathie fantastique.
Concerning the extreme distance
the mouse must go.
Mice eat paper because they like
to read, they eat soap because
they like to wash,
they do these things
because they are caught in
that great loop of nebulosity,
being alive just as they are.
They are the Essenes of concealment
in a pagoda of compassionate waste.
He who took the salt of the peanuts
is no more than a mouse.
He who stole an ounce of civet
to write King Lear.
What we think about when we think
about mice is how beautiful they are,
how they have found a way to live
cheaply and without tears,

how they make the same errors
Picasso might make, being
failing for a reason, and sent far
when comes trouble. Give them
the purple fantasy of your sock,
for who's who in hard times
is never known, and I do thinks they
taught the morning stars to sing together.
What the mouse says to survive
is so shockingly sweet and tender,
I think a single squeak evidence
for the existence of other minds,
and the iceman cometh to them too,
in their comfortable hole bye-bye.

UP ABOVE

I lived down below.
I read books, I listened to music,
I swam in deep dark waters
and shallow blue ones.
I watched the storm come over
the mountain and across the plain,
sometimes it was as close as the trees
which at that moment turned gray.
I felt things were near.
I felt them from afar.
You may ask, What are books? What is music?
Blasphemy, that's what they are.
You may ask what means blasphemy:
blasphemy means you are hearing the days,
they are falling, tears bring them no closer,
you love each one more than the rain,
which is spit from the gums of someone
playing table soccer up above.

PERIDOT

I awoke in an ecstasy.
The sky was the color of a cut lime
that had sat in the refrigerator
in a plastic container
for thirty-two days.
Fact-checkers, check.
I am happy.
Notice I speak in complete sentences.
Something I have not done since birth.
And the sky responds.

NARROW ROAD TO THE NORTH

Tonight is the night of the full untrustworthy moon.
My nails grow long while writing this.
Bashō thought a good life was spent picking up
horse chestnuts from off the ground.
Would he have picked up ordinary chestnuts?
I wonder why, since people weep at monuments,
they don't weep when they see ordinary stones.
When a stone is wedged between the cleats
of my boot, I remove it with my chopsticks.
Sometimes they break. Truly, it wakes you up.
But Bashō thought you had to see the whole pine.
He was also resigned to leaving his body behind
in a forsaken area, but stayed mostly in inns.
When Bashō wrote

> What a loss is here:
> Beneath the warrior's splendid helmet
> A chirping cricket

I thought he meant the man's brain.
I hate sandals. They have a mate.
Bashō did not travel alone, he had Sora.
He even wrote on his hat *I travel with a friend*.

When I first read the words
I thought he meant his sorrow.
Such are the changes of years
and my pitiful life compared to his
as any duck in flight can see.

WINGS OF LOVE

Doris keeps her doves in a basket
and lets them go
when someone gets married
and when someone dies.
Doris wears white hair and a white jacket
and uses the hand at the end of her arm
to point to the sky
when the wings go up.
They circle until they find each other,
they stay together for a while,
then they disperse.
It's called a release.
I'm not making any comparisons,
that's just the way things are—
an old lady, a bride, a few doves,
and a corpse.
Sometimes the priest
says a few words and the words go up,
they stay together for a while
and then they disperse.
Like a nightmare or a horse,
these events come and go.
Sometimes Doris breaks down
and goes out on a dark night

into the wildest country
to which she has access
and turns her flashlight
on herself—
blinded, she tries
to guess her surname.

DOLOROUS INTERLUDE

I was deeply troubled as I began my journey
to the end of the long smile. Out of
breath, like a clear drop of honey.
So a master walks before his superior
out of respect for the noisiness of feet,
so the world carries on its back
an albatross of music, and a swimmer divides
the sea by his strokes, and a child divides
the house with his cries. I in my natal casket,
and in the limo of my unconsciousness, began
to make some sense out of the embossed braille
of asphalt and mountains. I, the world's
oldest walking infant, toddled through
the empty days, and when a dolorous interlude
of diagonal rain fell, a river of tenderness
entered my heart, I bent down over the even
bigger baby of the world—you might think
I am too intelligent to believe what I'm saying
but I am not—and am bending still, it is
a position I must never break, so says
the supreme goddess of the void
smiling at me in white lipstick.

RUMORS OF EARTH

All things written feel a little terrified at first
as though come to destroy us
and with a loud voice
and all amazed
and immediately,
but making anything you have explored time,
and exploring time you have created the world,
even if it is only a little cairn of broken bricks
at the end of a rainbow.
Earthly splendor must have appeared long ago
and suffering established forever.
The tower said to the sun
See anyone coming?
The sun said Yes,
the past again coming tomorrow
issued with a clean gun
and the raw appearance of an oyster.
Rumors of Earth!
Still, my little injury,
we cannot do more at this point
than indicate a few minor principles
of maps in sand.
So long as morning is the chief authority,
at the sound of voices
the stars say nothing.

WHAT WENT YE OUT INTO MAY TO SEE?

At four in the morning
the earth began to smell,
black loam dilating the nostrils of irises
until they unfurled on the spot
and everything became charged
as if there were a loose horse
running down the beaten path.
The birds were driven crazy and said things
everyone wants to hear.
Meanwhile the town slept.
God knows what they dreamt.
Every girl over the age of twelve
drank and had a baby. Sometimes the fathers
would push the babies around the block
and give them a dirty shoe to suck on.
Every father over the age of nine smoked.
The only soul out on the streets was lost
in the middle of life, wandering and
weeping—no, wait, there was another one
screaming into his cell phone *You don't*
have any cool friends, Susan is a rubber tire
and Becky is fucking thirty and bangs guys
half her age, no, you don't, you don't
have any cool friends, so go fuck yourself, Alicia.
Everyone did terrible things with their cars,

driving them in a state of vagabondia

toward a mountain range

made of soft-serve.

Who knows the difference between man and nature?

Perhaps the river despises its own philosophy

and would stop if it could.

These are the questions of spring.

BLOODROOT

Here is a baby
the size of a rabbit
To her the world
is a virgin
Her eyes will pierce it
with unmeasured delight
while the tiny texture
of her eyelashes
will cast a lifelong
shadow, her pores
exude pleasant and
unpleasant smells,
and her toes squish
wet sand, mud, and
the toes of another
Who would have
her head? Who would
have her head?

Q & A

We notice you use the word *lonely*
in many of your poems, why is that?
Because Siegfried's difficult way to
Brunhild passes over eighty-nine pages
of rubble, of sticks, of stones, of
crushed glass, of minor boards, of
stinking creosote, of smashed skulls
and dead birds, of lost gloves, of
shards and turds and carpet remnants,
the whole way is paved with bottle caps
and flattened coins and the occasional
pair of broken spectacles, with tar
and rust and gravel and sand and brambles
and wire and old crumbly bricks and chunks
of mortar, with empty shotgun shells and
chewed-up pens and barfed-up bits of dinner
and cigar butts and snack wrappers and
plastic bottles tossed from cars, with rhino
whiskers and the inevitable single shoe without
laces, not to mention thousands of hooves
with the fur still on them and the animal bones
that have been eroding here for years
though the path more or less runs straight
and many of these things glint in the morning
sun, weirdly, why do you ask?

SUDDEN ADDITIONAL ENERGY

Star Light, Star Bright,
First Star I see tonight,
I wish I may, I wish I might,
have tranquillity of mind in sight.
And you there, little second star,
unnoticed in the dark blue corner,
what is my wish on you?
Over the years several friends
have had their kitchens remodeled,
a big deal at the time, yet they
never mention it now. The more I
look at you, the more I see their
marble countertops, lying sleek
and mentionless and forlorn.
I wish you, little marble,
would be my countertop, and I would
never stop talking about you!
I'm not in any kind of trance
as I wish this, I've not stepped
out of time, nor am I one with it.
All that stuff was with the first
star, but with you, little blue marble
second star, I am at home, completely
and safely at home. You can chop on me,

I can chop on you, why it is as if
I am a girl again, when my mother
had a bowl expressly shaped to
hold bananas, and simply
by putting grapes in it
I could get in trouble.

POEM WRITTEN BEFORE I WAS BORN

I decide on a piece of fruit.
In the month of July
in the middle of the month
in the middle of the day
in the month of that hour
I enter the internectarine world.
The stone is there, at last.
The seed is there, in that.
Now I will eat the rest of the flesh
of the nectarine fruit
the way all things eat each other
in the world at large,
a world I cannot enter
until I can repeat the ritual
described above
with my eyes closed
and in front of other people.

ELEGY FOR A GAME

Once I was on Earth
and I liked it.
I got to look at my toes
underwater. They looked bigger
than they were in real life.
As anyone can tell by looking at it
sugar is meaningless.
You are not supposed to stay in the hot tub
longer than ten minutes.
After that it is meaningless.
Like white poinsettias.
I mean at Christmas.
Maybe Christmas is meaningless too
but we used to pretend it was not
and I liked that.
It's pointless.
I don't actually know what a football looks like.
I think they have something to do with babies.
The man is carrying a baby across the field.
He is trying to save it.
It's hard.
Sometimes people die trying to do things.
That's okay.
There are things more important
than life or death.
I miss holding my breath.

WITH LOVE & DISREGARD

I was alive.
As you lay sleeping
with a freight train in your chest
I was not dead.
But because there are fewer people on earth
at night, I stepped out,
and the underground sentence of a mushroom
sent out a flower:
I found in the night many like me,
lonely and weird, with brown shoes,
who liked to eat with a fork,
earnest and capable of grasping
while vainly stumbling on the great way:
so may the unsurpassable unfabricated
wondrous method of time greet you squarely
so you may understand and instantly recognize
the mushroom that is my flower
and the vast underground network
of which it is the only sign.
And if ever you wish to call out
my summons is seven zeros, plus one
for the Operator, a pure clear ring
heard by the fires that burn all night
in their tin drums by the river.

PICKING UP PINECONES

I light a few candles, so
the moon is no longer alone.
My secret heart wakes
inside its draped cage
and cracks a song.
After a life of imagining,
I notice the ceiling.
It is painted blue
with a border of pinecones.
I've spent my life in a forest.
Picking up new things,
will it never end?

* * *

Grateful acknowledgment is made to the following journals, in which some of these poems first appeared: *The American Poetry Review, The Best American Poetry, Black Tongue Review, Conduit, Court Green, Crazyhorse, Forklift Ohio, Gulf Coast, Handsome, Hayden's Ferry Review, Headlamp, Indiana Review, iO: A Journal of New American Poetry, Jabberwock Review, The Kenyon Review, LIT, McSweeney's, New Ohio Review, The New Yorker, The New York Times, The Paris Review, Parthenon West Review, Poetry, Pool, Salt Hill, Storyscape, Sycamore Review, Tin House, Tuesday; An Art Project,* and *Washington Square Review.* Grateful acknowledgment is made to the following voices, who wandered briefly into some of these poems: Anselm Kiefer, Jules Olitski, John Keats, Joshua Beckman, Henry Darger, Nancy Eimers, Jon Cone, Meta Kušar, Abbas Kiarostami, Bede, Heraclitus, Wilhelm Müller, Larry Sutin, and Stephen Foster.